Thank you for
your support of
rescue pets!
xoxo

RESCUE PETS *of* BOSTON

AT HOME WITH THE CITY'S LUCKIEST PETS

BRITTANY BANG
&
LI WARD

Rescue Pets of Boston
At Home with the City's Luckiest Pets

By Brittany Bang & Li Ward
Photography, Design & Calligraphy by Li Ward

Text Copyright ©2013 Brittany Bang

Images Copyright ©2013 Li Ward, Fat Orange Cat Studio
www.FatOrangeCatStudio.com

Production Management by Jennifer Most Delaney
JMD Production

Published by Bang Enterprises
Email: Brittany@BangEnterprises.com

ISBN: 978-0-9899388-0-8 (Trade Hardcover)

Printed in the United States of America
by Worzalla Publishing Co.
www.worzalla.com

*Opposite: Bella
enjoying Boston*

Dedication

This book is dedicated to all of the amazing customers I met at Audrey's. You helped make my dream of opening up a neighborhood pet supply store become a reality and a truly amazing life experience. I will forever be grateful for your love and support over the years.

It was because of your compassion towards animals and your desire to build a better pet community in Boston which led us to be friends. Your friendship and encouragement to reach for the stars helped me get through the disappointment of closing my beloved store, and on to this next chapter in my life. - *Brittany*

I dedicate this book to my favorite rescue, VanBuren. I adopted you and your brother Bunny at the Buddy Dog Humane Society in Sudbury, Massachusetts with the intention of rescuing a different feline duo. But as I walked by the cage you and Bunny shared, you rubbed your orange head violently against the door. So there you had me.

I took a million pictures of you. When I decided to take photos of other people's pets for a living, I named my company "Fat Orange Cat Studio" after you. You were my wonderful purry furry friend and I sure do miss you. Thank you for choosing me. - *Li*

Letter To Our Readers

Thank you for taking the time to open our book, and your hearts, to rescue animals everywhere! While this book is about some wonderful rescue pets, it's also about some great humans, too. You see...

In 2009 Li shot a handsome Cavalier King Charles rescue named Floyd (featured in the book). Floyd's mom went to Back Bay Framery on Newbury to have her prints framed; there she met the owner Kerri and her rescue dog Sadie. Kerri enjoyed Li's work so much that she offered to display framed photographs of Floyd and other pets Li photographed throughout the store. It was a small established local business helping out a new small business owner!

One winter day in 2010 I stopped by Back Bay Framery, a store I have always loved for its hidden treasures, and immediately saw an amazing black & white photo of Floyd. I was in the process of opening Audrey's, a pet supply store just down the block, and had been searching for a local pet photographer to feature on the walls. Li's photos were exactly what I wanted - candid and beautiful - so I asked Kerri for the contact info. I called Li that very day.

Our working relationship grew into a friendship over our love of animals, cocktails and our appreciation for fellow local female entrepreneurs. Our businesses mingled; I hosted Li's first photography open house at Audrey's and we have collaborated on a number of projects since. And when I found out that Audrey's was going to have to close because a large retail developer was kicking us out, Li was one of my biggest supporters.

One day when having cocktails over lunch, I asked Li if she would consider working on a photography book with me. This book would be all about rescue pets. It would show that shelter animals are beautiful, special, unique and lovable - they were just waiting to find their forever homes. And this book would benefit the animals that still had not found a home: 100% of the proceeds would go to rescue groups and other animal-related charities. All I had to do was find a like-minded partner and photographer. Much to my amazement, Li agreed to work with me.

This project has been more eye-opening than we could have ever thought possible. Not only have we learned about ourselves and what we can accomplish, but we have reaffirmed our passion and commitment to supporting local small businesses. We have met so many wonderful people (and pets!) along the way and are so thankful to everyone who has participated. In supporting this home-grown project of ours, you have also supported so many deserving charities.

We thank you from the bottom of our hearts!

Sincerely,

Brittany (and Li)

our selected Charities

THE GIFFORD CAT SHELTER

THE GIFFORD CAT SHELTER IS A SANCTUARY LOCATED IN BRIGHTON, MASSACHUSETTS. THEIR MISSION IS TO TAKE IN HOMELESS CATS, PROVIDE THEM WITH HIGH QUALITY CARE IN A CAGE-LESS AND NO-KILL ENVIRONMENT, AND FIND HEALTHY AND LOVING PERMANENT HOMES FOR THEM. FOUNDED IN 1884 BY ELLEN GIFFORD, THE SHELTER WAS A PIONEER IN CREATING ENVIRONMENTS THAT DID NOT CONFINE ANIMALS TO SMALL, MOVEMENT-RESTRICTING CAGES. ORIGINALLY A SHELTER FOR ALL ANIMALS, GIFFORD IS NOW A SHELTER EXCLUSIVELY FOR CATS. www.GiffordCatShelter.org

FAIRY DOG PARENTS

WHAT BETTER WAY TO KEEP DOGS OUT OF SHELTERS THAN HELPING THEM STAY WITH THEIR OWNERS IN THE FIRST PLACE? FAIRY DOG PARENTS WAS FOUNDED IN 2009 TO PREVENT DOGS FROM BEING SURRENDERED TO SHELTERS BY FINANCIALLY STRAPPED OWNERS. THEY PROVIDE ASSISTANCE WITH FOOD, MEDICAL AND GENERAL WELLNESS NEEDS TO QUALIFIED RECIPIENTS IN MASSACHUSETTS. THIS SPECIAL ORGANIZATION PROVIDES HOPE AND KEEPS FAMILIES TOGETHER. www.FairyDogParents.org

ONE TAIL AT A TIME RESCUE

ONE TAIL AT A TIME RESCUE, BASED IN MASSACHUSETTS, IS A VOLUNTEER-ONLY ORGANIZATION. THEY RESCUE DOGS AND PUPPIES FROM HIGH-KILL SHELTERS IN THE RURAL SOUTH, AND BRING THEM UP NORTH. ALL THE RESCUED DOGS ARE PLACED WITH FOSTERS UNTIL THEY FIND THEIR FOREVER HOMES. ONE TAIL AT AT TIME STRIVES TO ADOPT OUT DOGS WHO ARE HEALTHY, HAPPY, AND FRIENDLY. www.OneTailAtATime.com

Audrey's Rescue Angels

Audrey's Rescue Angels was founded in 2013 to help create a more humane and sustainable world for all animals - including people - through education, advocacy, and promotion of respect and compassion. Audrey's Rescue Angels believes in people coming together to help build a better pet community by donating their time and raising awareness for animal welfare. www.AudreysRescueAngels.org

Animal Rescue League of Boston

In 1899 Boston social worker Anna Harris Smith wrote that "while getting dogs and cats off the street is work worth doing, the teaching of thoughtful kindness is the work that changes families, communities, and a nation." This philosophy launched the creation of an organization that has grown to respond to animals in need throughout Eastern Massachusetts and beyond. The Boston branch of the Animal Rescue League is located on Chandler Street in the South End. Many of the furry faces you see in "Rescue Pets of Boston" have once called the ARL their refuge before being rescued. www.ARLBoston.org

MSPCA-Angell

The MSPCA-Angell is a leader in animal protection and veterinary medicine, and provides direct hands-on care for thousands of animals each year. Founded in 1868, they are the second-oldest humane society in the United States. The mission of the MSPCA-Angell is to protect animals, advance their health and welfare, prevent cruelty, and work for a just and compassionate society. Please make sure to find some of the MSPCA's amazing staff members and their four-legged companions in this book! www.MSPCA.org

naturally good

For the last several months, we have crisscrossed Boston photographing some of the city's most beloved rescue pets - dogs, cats, rabbits, and fish alike. After everyone's hard work posing and smiling for the camera, we couldn't be more excited to share their images and stories with you.

These pets truly are the luckiest in Boston. We hope you will continue to think of pet adoption first!

Enjoy!

Emmie

Mini Beagle, aged 7

Rescued from Pay it Forward Animal Welfare Network in Henderson, Kentucky

Emmie is extremely social and is always making new friends while out and about in the Back Bay. It's probably because of her one eye - she looks like she's winking at you!

Mr. Boston

Jack Russell Terrier Mix, aged 3

Mr. Boston was rescued from the streets of Houston, Texas. his mom and littermates were found by a veterinary technician who worked in the same hospital as Mr. Boston's new mom. Lucky! Mr. Boston loves to sleep in. When his parents rise early for work, he jumps under the covers and refuses to come out.

Schooner

GOLDEN RETRIEVER, AGED 4
RESCUED FROM THE MSPCA, METHUEN

DESPITE BEING NAMED AFTER A BOAT
(PARENTS ARE AVID BOATERS), SCHOONER'S
FAVORITE MODE OF TRANSPORT IS VIA CAR.
HE WILL GET INTO ANY CAR, FAMILY CAR
OR NOT, AS LONG AS THE DOOR IS OPEN.
SCHOONER OCCASSIONALLY DRIVES INTO
THE OFFICE AT THE MSPCA IN JAMAICA
PLAIN, WHERE HIS MOM WORKS.

Otto

ORANGE TABBY, AGED 5
RESCUED FROM THE MSCPA, BOSTON

OTTO, NAMED FOR KEVIN KLINE'S
CHARACTER IN A FISH CALLED WANDA, IS A
CAT-DOG. HE SITS FOR TREATS (PREFERS DOG
TREATS) AND GREETS YOU AT THE DOOR. HE
SOMETIMES ACCOMPANIES HIS MOM AND
DOG BROTHER SCHOONER TO WORK.

Notice to Employees: Dog/Cat in the Office

My names is: *Otto (cat) + Schooner (dog)*

My owner is: *Laura Hay* My owner's supervisor: *Alice Bruce*

I am here because: *Photo Shoot*

I am:

☑ Friendly: Say hello!
☐ Shy: Please ask before petting me
☐ Scared: I would not like to interact please do not enter

Other instructions: *We love EVERYONE!!*

Nota para todos los Empleados: Perro/Gato en el Lugar de trabajo

Mi nombre es:

Mi dueño es: _____ Mi supervisor del dueño es:

Estoy aquí porque:

Yo Soy:

☐ Amistoso: ¡Diga hola!
☐ Tímido: Por favor pregunte antes de acariciarme
☐ Asustado: No quisiera estar incomunicandome por favor no entre

Luna

Husky, aged 7
Adopted from Big Fluffy Dog Rescue
Nashville, Tennessee

Luna was adopted by her foster parents who inevitably could not resist making her a permanent part of their family. She was named "Luna" because her one blue eye looks like the moon. Luna is gentle with the household cats, patient with children, and is always eager to roll over for belly rubs.

Usagi Biscotti

LIONHEAD RABBIT, AGED 2

USAGI IS JAPANESE FOR "BUNNY". BISCOTTI MEANS "TWICE-BAKED" AND SHE WAS PREVIOUSLY OWNED TWICE. USAGI WAS RESCUED FROM A BAKER WHO COULD NO LONGER CARE FOR HER. SHE LOVES MUNCHING ON CILANTRO AND CARROTS, AND ENJOYS PLAYING WITH HER CAT AND DOG.

Miss Kitty von Teese

BOMBAY/ORIENTAL, AGED 3

MISS KITTY CAME FROM A CAT RESCUE IN QUEENS, NEW YORK. HER DAD DESCRIBES HER AS AN EPIC ROYAL BEAUTY AND A SWANKY REBEL. HER TWO BEST FRIENDS ARE A BUNNY AND A DOG.

Mack

Dogue de Bordeaux, aged 5½ years
built like a Mack truck

Mack's story of courage began after being rescued by the Atlantic Veterinary Hospital in Marblehead. He was abused before being rescued, but soon became a very important part of his new family's life.

Mack is no longer with us after recently losing his battle with cancer. To the end he remained a brave dog and a wonderful friend.

Peetie

TABBY CAT, AGED 3

ADOPTED FROM THE ANIMAL RESCUE LEAGUE IN BOSTON,
SHY LITTLE PEETIE LOVES LOOKING OUT THE WINDOW AND
CHASING HIS TAIL AGGRESSIVELY SEVERAL TIMES A DAY. HE
SHARES A HOME WITH HIS FELLOW RESCUE KITTY MIA IN
THE BACK BAY.

Sadie

Beagle/Basset Hound/Shepherd mix, aged 7½
Adopted from the Northeast Animal Shelter
Salem, Massachusetts

Sadie is her owner's constant companion and is most happy being just a few feet away. She is the proud owner of The Back Bay Framery, a beautiful framing store on Newbury Street. She is there every work day, greeting patrons or snoozing by her owner's feet.

Houdini

Turkish Van, aged 15
Adopted from Spay and Save, Philadelphia

Houdini was rescued from the streets of South Philly. His rescuer said that he was with a pack of alley cats but was the only one who came running to her when she called! Houdini's most notable feature is his two different colored eyes. He will talk your ear off, especially when he wants chicken. Houdini lives with his mom and dad in Arlington, Massachusetts.

Hobbes

Tabby, aged 8
Adopted from the
Animal Rescue League,
Boston

Hobbes is a lovable fat
orange cat with a feisty
side. His ears are too
big for his head. He
is asthmatic, but that
doesn't hold him back.
He has an inhaler!

Hazel

Tortie, aged 8
Adopted from the
Animal Rescue League,
Boston

Shy, sweet Hazel drools
when she is happy. She is
happiest when sitting on
an open window sill. So
when you see her there,
you can be sure she's
drooling.

Van

Beagle Mix, aged 2

Rather than bark to communicate, Van yawns, grumbles and makes various strange noises! He was adopted from the Animal Rescue Network of New England in Pelham, New Hampshire and now makes his home in Arlington, Massachusetts.

Thatcher
LHASA APSO, AGED 8

THATCHER WAS RESCUED FROM LHASA
HAPPY HOMES IN LOS ANGELES. HE
HAS MANY NICKNAMES, INCLUDING
SPICY GRANDPA, WOLFGANG, PEKING
DUCK...THE LIST GOES ON! HE LIVES IN
BRIGHTON WITH HIS FELLOW RESCUE
BROTHER DINKIE.

Dinkie
MALTIPOO, AGED 3

DINKIE WAS FOSTERED BY A VOLUNTEER
FOR LHASA HAPPY HOMES RESCUE.
HE WAS RECOVERING FROM SEVERE
PNEUMONIA AND WAS NURSED BACK TO
HEALTH. HIS FOSTER MOM FELT THAT
AFTER GOING THROUGH SO MUCH WITH
THIS LITTLE PUP, SHE HAD TO KEEP HIM!
DINKIE LOVES PLAYING BALL MORE THAN
ANYTHING.

"Saving one dog will not change the world, but surely for that one dog the world will change forever." - Karen Davison

Sampson

Domestic Shorthair, aged 4
Rescued from the Animal
Rescue League, Boston

Sampson is shy around others
but is an extraordinarily
affectionate kitty. His favorite
snack is tuna fish, and he
loves a good game of fetch.

Sofia

Domestic Longhair, Aged 2
Rescued from the MSPCA Boston

Sofia lives in a beautiful wine shop called Bauer Wine & Spirits, and is the 3rd in a line of distinguished store cats who have all been rescued. People who come into the shop are so fond of Ms. Sofia that they insist on taking her picture. It is not a surprise that she has her own Facebook page.

Griffin

Coonhound/Beagle mix, aged 3

Griffin loves people. At the
dog park, he spends more time
getting pet by humans than
playing with other dogs.
Whenever Griffin goes for a
walk with his owner, he looks
up every once in awhile as if
to say, "Don't worry Mom, I've
got you!"

Smirnoff

Domestic shorthair, aged 4
Rescued from the Animal
Rescue League, Boston

Smirnoff got his name because of his love for chasing bottle caps. He will sit, lay down, and roll over for a treat!

Bacardi

Domestic shorthair, aged 3½
Rescued from the Animal
Rescue League, Boston

Bacardi loves to steal people's seats at parties! He is being clicker trained and at press time, is able to sit up for a treat.

Copley

Maltese, aged 3
Adopted from the Animal Rescue League
Boston

Copley is the "mayor" of the dog park. He
loves every person and every dog he sees
and insists on greeting them all. He is a
fearless and a happy little dog!

Jane

Pit Bull, aged 8
Rescued from the
Philadelphia Animal Welfare Society

Jane was mismarked as a male and was scheduled
to be put down as the shelter was over-populated
with pit bulls. Jane's mother, a vet from the
Back Bay Veterinary, saved her life and now she
happily makes her home in Medford.

"*Money will buy a pretty good dog, but it won't buy the wag of his tail.*" - Josh Billings

Mia

Tortie, aged 15
adopted from Alliance for Animals in
Arlington, Massachusetts

Mia was adopted from a feral colony
when she was 3. She was missing patches
of fur, had no teeth, and was eating out
of cans. Now, she is the elegant lady of a
Back Bay penthouse and knows how exotic
she is! Mia means "mine" in Spanish.

Junebug

Pug, aged 9

Junebug was a Hurricane Katrina pup who was never reunited with her family. She was adopted through a Louisiana rescue. None of the other names seemed to fit until one day she was caught sniffing a junebug! She has lost 80% of her eyesight but that doesn't stop her from being adventurous and exploring her new neighborhood of South Boston.

Belle

Beagle, aged 14
Loves Dumpsters

Kyra

Coonhound, aged 11
Loves butterscotch
ice cream

Circe

Coonhound, aged 8
Loves dead fish

Belle and Kyra (the one pictured howling) were strays, and Circe was dumped as a puppy in the woods. Their endless loyalty, love for people and joy for life is apparent when they go sailing, hiking, exploring the city, or making the rounds at nursing homes. Their owners say, "We are very thankful for our crew. They keep us safe and we will always have them and their paw prints in our hearts!"

Zelda
Lab/Boxer, aged 3
Adopted from Rescue Angels Adoption Agency
in Tennessee

Zelda was named after the wife of author F. Scott Fitzgerald. She likes to move your shoes around when you're not looking. This lucky girl currently lives in Dorchester next to what was the first chocolate factory in America - the Baker Chocolate Factory!

Chippa & Frisky

GUINEA PIGS, AGED 2 AND 4
ADOPTED FROM THE
ANIMAL RESCUE LEAGUE, BOSTON

CHIPPA'S FAVORITE FOOD IS CRANBERRIES.
HE IS INSEPARABLE FROM HIS BROTHER.

FRISKY'S PREFERRED MEAL INVOLVES
CARROTS AND DANDELIONS. HE ALSO
ENJOYS HIS BROTHER'S COMPANY.

THIS LUCKY PAIR COMES FROM A LARGE
FAMILY OF RESCUES THAT INCLUDES THREE
DOGS - BELLE, CIRCE, AND KYRA - AND
MR. FISH, ALL OF WHOM ARE IN THIS
BOOK.

Butternut

FRENCH BULLDOG, AGED 4 MONTHS
ADOPTED FROM FurKidsRUS IN OKLAHOMA

NAMED AFTER THE BUTTERNUT MUNCHKIN FROM
DUNKIN DONUTS, BUTTERNUT THE FRENCHIE IS NEWLY
ADOPTED AND ALREADY A CITY BUTTERFLY! HE STOPS TO
SAY HELLO TO EVERYONE DURING WALKS IN HIS SOUTH
END NEIGHBORHOOD, MAKING FRIENDS WITH HUMAN
AND FURRY RESIDENTS ALIKE. IT IS NO WONDER THAT
THEY ALL REFER TO HIM BY NAME!

Captain Mozzarella Drumstick

ORANGE TABBY, AGED 5
RUNNING AROUND ON THREE LEGS

CAPTAIN WAS BROUGHT INTO THE ANIMAL HOSPITAL IN
SUDBURY, MASSACHUSETTS WHEN HE WAS JUST 1 DAY
OLD. HIS LEG WAS BADLY MANGLED AND HIS MOTHER HAD
ABANDONED HIM. HE WAS TO BE PUT DOWN BUT INSTEAD
THE VETERINARIAN PERFORMED SURGERY TO REMOVE HIS
LEG AND CLEAN HIS WOUNDS. THEN SHE ADOPTED HIM!
CAPTAIN NOW LOVES LIFE AND HIS FAVORITE FOODS ARE
BANANAS, CANTALOUPE, AND CORN.

Oliver

Cavalier King Charles Spaniel, Aged 6

Oliver was taken out of an abusive home in Connecticut. Now he loves spending time with Mom & Dad in their South End home, and going on Cape Cod boat rides in the summer. Oliver even goes clamming and helps dig some up himself!

Brynnley

Chihuahua Mix, aged 3

Brynn was rescued from the Northeast Animal Shelter in Salem, Massachusetts by way of Puerto Rico. She was a Sato - a stray dog found on Puerto Rico's infamous Dead Dog Beach when she was just a puppy. Now Brynn is happy to be living the high life with her mom in the heart of Beacon Hill.

Figaro

Norwegian Forest Cat, aged 7
Adopted from the Animal Rescue League,
Boston

The road to Figaro's forever home was long & winding. Found as a stray and brought to the ARL of Boston, this handsome fellow was so stressed to be caged that he hissed, bit, and scratched nearly every staff member & volunteer he encountered, thus spending more time in quarantine than on the adoption floor. He was adopted out one time, only to be returned. Finally he was rescued by an ARL volunteer who could resist him no longer. Today, warmly ensconced in his South End home, Figaro (aka The Big Fig) pays it forward by helping foster the kittens that come through, including Bingley who is in this book. After overseeing bottle feedings, he grooms the kittens, conducts pouncing lessons, & shows them correct litterbox usage. Figaro's resilience is an inspiration to us all!

Bingley

Mackerel Longhair
nevertheless referred to as a Maine Coon,
King of the Forest, aged 3½
Adopted from the Animal Rescue League,
Boston

When Bingley's owners first met him, he was but a few weeks old, just weaned off the bottle, and sat in the palm of their hands comfortably. Because he seemed so pleased to meet everyone's acquaintance, he was named "Bingley" after the character from his mom's favorite book, *Pride & Prejudice.* Bingley enjoys fetching crumpled pieces of paper, pushing nickels under the rug, and playing with water. If there's an overturned water bowl, then there's a Bingley in the house!

Argus

SATO, AGED 2

GUS, AS HE IS KNOWN, WAS RESCUED FROM PUERTO RICO VIA THE ANIMAL RESCUE LEAGUE AND ALL SATO RESCUE. HE WAS NAMED AFTER ULYSSES' DOG FROM *THE ODYSSEY*. GUS HAD SEVERE SEPARATION ANXIETY BUT WORKED THROUGH IT TO COMPLETE HIS AKC CANINE GOOD CITIZEN TITLE! GUS LIVES BY THE SEA AND LOVES PLAYING FETCH ON THE BEACHES OF WINTHROP, MASSACHUSETTS, WHERE HE MAKES HIS HOME.

"A house is not a home without a dog." - Unknown

Boo Radley

Domestic Longhair, aged 3
Named after the owner's
favorite book character

Boo Radley was rescued from
the CASAS Animal Shelter in
Provincetown, Massachusetts.
Boo was sent to the CASAS
after surviving a shelter fire
in West Virginia. He was one
of the very few who did. His
meow is now a little squeaky
beacuse of all the smoke
inhalation he experienced
in the fire. He now lives a
comfortable, smoke-free life
with his parents in Allston.

Misha

CHIHUAHUA MIX, AGED 15
ADOPTED FROM THE MSPCA BOSTON

MISHA WAS ADOPTED WHEN SHE WAS
ABOUT 6 YEARS OLD. SHE HAD BEEN
SEVERELY ABUSED AND NEGLECTED,
AND SPENT OVER A YEAR WITH A
FOSTER FAMILY UNTIL SHE COULD
STAND ON HER OWN. YOU WOULD
NEVER KNOW OF HER TOUGH PAST
BECAUSE OF HER CALM AND CARING
TEMPERAMENT. SHE LOVES AND
TRUSTS UNCONDITIONALLY.

Mason

CHIHUAHUA MIX, AGED 6
ADOPTED FROM THE ANIMAL RESCUE
LEAGUE, BOSTON

MASON WAS A BEHAVIORAL SPECIAL
NEEDS ADOPTION. HE FAILED ALL
TESTS BUT HIS OWNERS KNEW THERE
WAS SOMETHING SPECIAL ABOUT HIM.
THEY TOOK MASON TO "FINISHING
SCHOOL" FOR 1.5 YEARS WHERE HE
EARNED "MOST IMPROVED STUDENT."
GO MASON!

BASSET HOUND/GOLDEN RETRIEVER MIX, AGED 3
ADOPTED FROM THE NORTHEAST ANIMAL SHELTER
SALEM, MASSACHUSETTS

Daisy

DAISY WAS RESCUED AT 7 MONTHS OLD. SHE HAD BRIGHT YELLOW
PUPPY FUR ON HER HEAD WHICH MADE HER MOM & DAD THINK OF
A BRIGHT AND SUNNY DAISY. NOW AT HOME IN THE SOUTH END,
DAISY'S UNIQUE SHAPE MAKES HER THE MOST MEMORABLE DOG ON
THE BLOCK. IT IS HER SWEET DISPOSITION AND LOVE OF ALL THINGS
HUMAN THAT MAKES HER ONE OF A KIND!

Jean-Benoit Aubrey

Tuxedo Domestic Shorthair,
aged 6 months
Adopted from the MSPCA
Boston

Since Benoit has one eye, his
mom named him after a pirate.
Jean-Benoit Aubrey was a
sympathetic, romantic French
pirate of the 17th Century,
and that name seemed to
fit the bill! Benoit, as he is
known, loves to play fetch. He
does not let his one eye slow
him down.

Benoit runs around with his
cat sisters in a big house in
Chestnut Hill.

"Thousands of years ago, cats were worshipped as gods. Cats have never forgotten this." - Unknown

Gabby

Beagle mix (but no one believes it!), aged 3

Rescued from the Puppy Railroad Rescue in New Hampshire, Gabby can impersonate many animals. She can jump like a squirrel, crawl like a snake, stand like a prairie dog, run like a deer, love like a human. Just like the human members of her Italian family, Gabby will do anything for a meatball!

Isabella
DOMESTIC SHORTHAIR, AGED 5

ISABELLA WAS RESCUED IN HONDURAS WHEN HER NOW MOM WAS IN THE PEACE CORPS. ISABELLE HAD 4 LITTERS (14 KITTENS!) BEFORE SHE WAS TAKEN ON A 7-HOUR BUS TRIP TO THE NEAREST VET JUST TO GET SPAYED. HAPPILY MANY OF HER KITTENS WENT TO OTHER PEACE CORPS VOLUNTEERS, AND 3 MADE THEIR WAY TO THE US!

Riley
DOMESTIC MEDIUMHAIR, AGED 7

RILEY, RESCUED FROM THE MSPCA IN BOSTON, WAS NAMED AFTER THE BASKETBALL COACH PAT RILEY. SHE LOVES OPEN WINDOWS AND THE FRESH AIR!

Scooby
STREET DOG, AGED 4

SCOOBY WAS FOUND IN HONDURAS AS A PUPPY, COVERED IN FLEAS, ALMOST FURLESS, AND SUFFERING FROM BLOAT DUE TO WORMS. THANKS TO HIS NEW MOM HE WAS NURSED BACK TO HEALTH AND IT WAS LOVE FROM THE START. SCOOBY IS BILINGUAL, RESPONDING TO BOTH ENGLISH AND SPANISH.

"The greatness of a nation and its moral progress can be judged by the way its animals are treated." - Ghandi

Mr. Fish

Beta Fish, aged 3
Adopted from the
Animal Rescue League,
Boston

Mr. Fish enjoys getting new plants, flowers, and seashells in his bowl. He makes himself comfortable in any setting, as long as he is in his home tank!

Clara
Belle of the Ball

Pug, aged 8
Rescued from the Pug Rescue
of New England

Even though Clara doesn't like to swim, she loves to walk everyday along the docks of the Charlestown Navy Yard, where she lives. She even has her own life jacket and enjoys boating.

Reese

Maine Coon/Tortie, aged 4

Reese was rescued from the Sterling Cat Shelter in Sterling, massachusetts. She was named "Reese" because her fur is the color of Reese's Pieces. She loves mint gum, looking at pictures of her boyfriend Bingley, and being a new mom to the household's recent adoption of two rescue kittens (who may be featured in our next book...)!

Zeus

PIT BULL/MASTIFF, AGED 2

ZEUS IS A BIG GOOF BALL. HE MAY
BE WAY OVER 100 POUNDS BUT
HE IS TERRIFIED OF PLASTIC BAGS
AND HIS 14-POUND SISTER! ZEUS
WAS RESCUED FROM THE BOSTON
ANIMAL CONTROL SHELTER IN
ROSLINDALE, MASSACHUSETTS.

Floyd

Cavalier King Charles Spaniel, aged 4
Rescued from Ladybugs K9 Rescue
Ohio

Floyd's owners say that he rescued them from a tough time and place so much more than they rescued him. He is a true "rescue dog" indeed. A wagging tail does not suffice. Floyd wags his entire body!

Floyd lives with his two cat siblings in the heart of Charlestown. They remain unimpressed with him.

"All his life he tried to be a good person.
Many times, however, he failed. For after all,
he was only human. He wasn't a dog."
- Charles M. Schulz

Charlie

Tabby, aged 4
Adopted from the MSPCA, Boston

When Charlie does something "bad," like climbing on the kitchen counters, she argues back, making fast little mews in protest! Charlie's parents are avid hockey fans and so she has own her Bruins jersey that she wears during game time. Together they live in South Boston.

Scooter

Black Lab/Dachshund hound mix, aged 4
Rescued from PAWS of Dale Hollow
Tennessee

Scooter was found abandoned in a box on the side of a Tennesse road. His owner decided to adopt a black dog because they are the first to be overlooked in a shelter. Scooter enjoys sleeping under blankets even if it's 99 degrees!

Simone

Yellow Lab/Whippet/Pit Bull mix, aged 5
Rescued from Golden Huggs Dog Rescue
Tennessee

Simone was found in a ditch with her litter mates before being transferred to a Rhode Island foster family. Simone loves her people and is incredibly loyal. She even has her own bed in her mom's studio so that she can keep her company all day.

*"A dog need not be a purebred
to be pure of heart."* - Unknown

Toby

COCKER SPANIEL/SHIH TZU
AGED 6
RESCUED FROM THE GOOD DOG
RESCUE IN TENNESSEE

TOBY WAS NICKNAMED "SIR
TOBY" BY HIS RESCUE BECAUSE
OF HIS DIGNIFIED NATURE,
HOWEVER, HE WILL DO JUST
ABOUT ANYTHING FOR SOME
TURKEY. HIS LIFE-LONG GOAL
IS TO CATCH A SQUIRREL.

Harriet

UNDOMESTICATED LONGHAIR, AGE UNKNOWN

HARRIET IS A STUNNING FERAL CAT WHO LIVES
IN THE BACKYARD WITH HER FELLOW FERAL
FRIEND BUDDY, WHO WOULD NOT JOIN HER
IN THIS PHOTO SHOOT. HARRIET IS PUNCTUAL
ABOUT MEAL TIMES ON THE BACK PORCH, AND
IS NOT SO FERAL THAT SHE WON'T SAY HELLO
TO HER DOMESTICATED BROTHER HOBBES
AT THE DOOR. WHEN SHE IS NOT HIDING
IN SHRUBBERY, HARRIET ENJOYS CHASING
CHIPMUNKS INTO THE POOL.

Dill Pickle

GOOFY NAME FOR A GOOFY DOG
PIT BULL, AGED 6

DILL IS VERY GRATEFUL FOR HIS NEW LIFE. HE CAME FROM A SITUATION THAT WAS BAD AS IT COULD BE - FORCED TO FIGHT WITH OTHER DOGS, LOCKED IN A SMALL AND DIRTY CRATE FOR HOURS, DAYS AT A TIME, AND STARVED. BUT ONCE HE FOUND HIS NEW LIFE, HE NEVER LOOKED BACK!

DILL'S "GRANDMOTHER" WAS NERVOUS ABOUT PIT BULLS, BUT AFTER MEETING THIS SWEET BOY HER ATTITUDE TOWARDS THE BREED WAS FOREVER CHANGED. SHE NOW EDUCATES OTHERS ABOUT BREED SPECIFIC LEGISLATION. CLEARLY MR. PICKLE IS A GREAT AMBASSADOR FOR HIS BREED. WAY TO GO DILL!

Max

Tuxedo cat, aged 6

Max was found wandering a school playground with no tags. His new mom scooped him up and he has been living the good life ever since. Max loves to rub noses with his dog sister Lulu. They make a cozy home together in Boston's Back Bay.

Isabelle Roo

MINI DASCHUND/RAT TERRIER, AGED 7

ISABELLE WAS FOUND ON THE
ROADSIDE OF A BUSY HIGHWAY IN
HOUSTON, TEXAS. ISABELLE JUMPS
LIKE A KANGAROO AND HAS A LARGE
VOCABULARY, EXPESSING EXACTLY WHAT
SHE WANTS!

Watson

JACK RUSSELL TERRIER MIX, AGED 4½
RESCUED FROM THE SPCA MOBILE
ADOPTION PROGRAM

WHEN WATSON LOOKS AT HIS MOM YOU
CAN SEE HIS LOVE AND AFFECTION FOR
HER. HE IS AN AVID SQUIRREL HUNTER.

Ruby

TORTIE, AGED 8

RUBY SHOWED UP AT HER OWNER'S
APARTMENT ONE NIGHT AND NEVER LEFT.
HER BEST FRIEND IS HER DOG BROTHER. THEY
WRESTLE, PLAY, AND GIVE EACH OTHER KISSES.

Heidi

Coton de Tulear Mix, aged 8
Rescued from Tennessee via
Forever Homes Rescue
New England

When Heidi was rescued she
had very advanced cataracts
in both eyes and was thus
effectively blind. Her new
parents got her the surgery
she needed. Heidi was very
patient and resilient through
the operation and post-op.
Now that she's able to see, her
confidence and personality
have bloomed!

Sally

Hound Mix, aged 6
Rescued from Triangle Beagle Rescue
Durham, North Carolina

Sally is a dog's dog. She is everything
people love (and love to hate!) about dogs:
she's a cuddler, a slobberer, and a loyal,
naughty, stinky, sweetheart of a girl! Sally
makes mischief with her dog brother in
Beacon Hill.

Tess

TUXEDO DOMESTIC SHORTHAIR, AGED 6

ADOPTED FROM THE TIGERLILY CAT RESCUE
IN SANTA CLARITA, CALIFORNIA, TESS WAS
NAMED AFTER THE BOSTON RED SOX'S BALL
GIRL AS A TRIBUTE TO HER OWNER'S HOME
TOWN AND HER LOVE OF BASEBALL. TESS IS
A SHY BUT LOVING GIRL AND IS EXTREMELY
PATIENT WITH HER HUMAN BABY BROTHER,
EVEN THOUGH HE LIKES TO PULL HER TAIL.

SHE SHARES HER LITTERBOX WITH YOGI,
ALSO FEATURED IN THIS BOOK.

Yogi

Maine Coon, aged 5½
Adopted from Tigerlily Cat Rescue
Santa Clarita, California

To even out the household, Yogi's parents named him after the New York Yankees ballplayer Yogi Berra. Yogi can be feisty at times but he can't wait to get up on his parents' laps at the end of a long day. He enjoys showing off his massive belly.

Doobie

American Bulldog mix, aged 8
Adopted from the Humane Society of
Boulder Valley, Colorado

Doobie is extremely compassionate and
worries about his owners all the time. He
may look tough but he is a very sensitive
guy! Doobie is scared of thunder and
loud noises, but luckily has his pal Layla
to hold on to.

Layla

Domestic Longhair, aged 6
Adopted from the Humane Society of
Boulder Valley, Colorado

Layla loves her dog brother Doobie more
than anyone. She was a little kitten
when they first met but now she is in
charge! Layla and Doobie live with their
parents in a historic converted hotel in
the Back Bay.

"Animals are such agreeable friends - they ask no questions; they pass no criticisms."
- George Eliot

Scarlett

Carolina Dog, aged 2½

Scarlett was adopted in New Hampshire through a Kentucky-based rescue league. A people-person all around, Scarlett will climb into her owner's chair while she's in it, and watch her as she works. Scarlett lives with her dog sister Bea in West Roxbury.

Bea

CHIWINI, AGED 2½

BEA IS A RESCUE FROM A PUPPY
MILL IN SOUTH CAROLINA. BEA'S
MOST ENDEARING QUALITY IS HER
BODY WIGGLE. IT IS PARTICULARLY
NOTICEABLE AROUND MEAL TIME!

Chance

Boxer/Beagle mix, aged 9
Rescued from the Orlando Humane Society/
SPCA of Central Florida

Chance inspired his mom to quit her job in corporate america to work in an animal rescue. He has his own team of humans, named "Chancey's Angels," who raise money on behalf of organizations like the MSPCA and the Quincy Animal Shelter. Mom's office is at the MSPCA Boston where Chance can be seen lounging by her feet.

Love me...
Love my Dog
Chance

Tuxedo cat, aged 9 *Sassy*

Sassy's mom rescued her outside of a Bennigan's restaurant. She was a malnourished 9-month-old stray. Today Sassy is a food thief - she steals her dog brother Chance's food and runs!

Tosh & Marley

Domestic Shorthairs, aged 3½

Tosh & Marley were rescued in Weymouth, Massachusetts. Along with their littermates, they were abandoned at only a few weeks old. Now they live the good life on Newbury Street! Tosh is known as the Gentle Giant with an Old Soul. Marley is the playful one - a kitten at heart and a Momma's boy.

Maddie

Lab Mix, aged 4½

Maddie was rescued from a high-kill shelter in Zanesville, Ohio with the help of Akron Canine Rescue Angels. Her favorite hobbies are playing tug, wrestling, and swimming in her own private pool.

Her best friend in the world is her orange tabby cat.

"Time spent with a cat is never wasted."
- Colette

Special Thanks

Both authors would like to thank Rob Charlton (Captain's Dad) of Goosefish Press for introducing us to our project coordinator, Jen Delaney of JMD Production.

Jen, your guidance, advice, and genuine love for book printing has helped us make this book concept into a reality. Your time and efforts are more appreciated than you will ever know.

Thank you so much to Colleen Ellse of Letter & Lark for helping create the perfect illustration for our project.

From L.W.
Thank you Sarah Bianculli (and mom to Scooter & Simone) for your guidance on the ever-important selection of fonts!

A big shout out to Marna Terry (Figaro's mom) for your installation of "Kittens and Wine Friday" where I play with the kittens you're fostering and you pour me wine. You are a true friend and protector of all cats in need!

Thank you Dan for staying up late and reworking my jumbled sentences into something more readable. Thank you for getting take-out and letting Britt and me drink all your favorite beers.

To all my pet and wedding photography clients - thank you for your enthusiastic support of this project. We wouldn't have a book without you!

Brittany, you waited until that 3rd round of drinks before asking me if I would do this "crazy" project with you. But you were so sad to have just lost your store - how could I say no? Honestly, I would never work this hard for no pay for anyone else. It's been such a privilege to be your friend and biz partner. Next round's on me.

From B.B.
Thank you to my 3 biggest fans for supporting me throughout this project. To my husband, Brad, and my parents, Karen & Jens - thank you for your love and guidance.

When I was at a very big crossroad in my life you helped remind me that I am an entrepreneur at heart and there is actually nothing wrong with that. Thank you, Mr. Tom Harrison, for being such an inspiration towards my career – whether you know it or not!

Other than myself, there is only one other person I would want to work for and that's you, Jason Sweeney. You have always been there for me as a friend and mentor and I thank you for sharing so much knowledge with me.

Thank you to Mary Donovan, the best English teacher around, for editing the contents of this book. I didn't give you a lot of turnaround time and thank you for your help, as always.

To my animal rescue family – Thank you Dana, Kathleen, Raina, Laura, and Heather for making me a small part of your lives and for the work you do on behalf of animals everywhere. You inspire me each and every day.

Thank you to Elaine and Wiggly Butt Designs for always helping me and my business. Your heart is amazing and I am so lucky we are friends.

Lastly, to my photography partner – Li, I wish there were more words to express my gratitude but we'll have to leave it at "Thank You."

Li

BIOGRAPHIES

LI WARD IS A BOSTON-BASED WEDDING & PET PHOTOGRAPHER. AFTER YEARS OF SNAPPING PHOTOS OF HER TWO RESCUE CATS, BUNNY & VANBUREN, LI STARTED HER BUSINESS FAT ORANGE CAT STUDIO IN 2009. ORIGINALLY SPECIALIZING IN PET PHOTOGRAPHY, SHE BEGAN PHOTOGRAPHING WEDDINGS (HUMANS) SOON AFTER.

LI NAMED FAT ORANGE CAT STUDIO AFTER HER WONDERFUL ORANGE TABBY VANBUREN AND ALL THE MANY PLUMP CATS SHE HAS HAD THROUGHOUT HER LIFE. HER PET IMAGES HAVE BEEN FEATURED IN *THE NEW YORK TIMES* AND *BOSTON MAGAZINE*. SHE WAS AWARDED "BOSTON'S BEST CALLIGRAPHER" BY *THE IMPROPER BOSTONIAN* IN 2011, AND NAMED ONE OF "30 RISING STARS OF WEDDING PHOTOGRAPHY" BY *RANGEFINDER MAGAZINE* IN 2012. HER WEDDING WORK HAS BEEN FEATURED IN *BOSTON WEDDINGS MAGAZINE*, *THE KNOT BOSTON*, AND *STYLE ME PRETTY*, TO NAME A FEW.

SHE LIVES WITH HER HUSBAND DAN AND THEIR TWO CATS, BUNNY AND BINGLEY, IN BOSTON'S SOUTH END. YOU CAN SEE SOME OF HER DOG CLIENT PORTRAITS AT THE PET-FRIENDLY SOUTH END BUTTERY BAKERY & CAFE.

Brittany

I was attending school at Emerson College when I brought home my smushy-faced bulldog. I named her after the most beautiful person I could think of, Audrey Hepburn. Audrey and I had wonderful adventures together before I lost her to cancer in 2007.

Though I worked in corporate America for many years, first as a client services manager for the Boston Red Sox, and then as a franchise consultant for Ben & Jerry's, I have always been an entrepreneur at heart. I opened my first business in the summer of 2010 called Audrey's Pet Supply & Services with the support of my husband, Brad, and my parents, Karen & Jens. Audrey's goal was to cater to pet owners living in and around the heart of Boston with everyday items - food, treats, toys, even walks. We were located on historic Newbury Street and within only two short years of opening, we were named named one of the "Top Ten Businesses in Boston" by *Boston Magazine*.

My time at Audrey's was cut far too short when a real estate developer purchased the building we were in and increased our rent by an exorbitant amount. We were left with no choice but to close.

Though our customers encouraged us to open another Audrey's location, I began to reevaluate what really made me happy. From day one, Audrey's tried to raise awareness for shelter pets and other animal-related causes that were near and dear to my heart. For a small business we tried to make as big of an impact in our community as we possibly could with various fundraisers and sponsored charitable events. What I loved most about my store was having this loyal customer base who shared and promoted this vision of building a better pet community.

During the three years I owned Audrey's, I learned more lessons than most do in a lifetime. With the store's closing I realized I wanted to preserve the relationships that I had built. I believe in the power of small businesses and the idea that we can all make a big difference in our community. As Audrey Hepburn once said, "As you grow older, you will discover you have two hands, one for helping yourself, the other for helping others."

I am currently the President of Bang Enterprises and look forward to growing and developing my own company. I am also the proud Founder and President of Audrey's Rescue Angels which is a non-profit I started after the close of my store. It is dedicated to building a better pet community through local activism and education. My husband, Brad, is my biggest source of strength and stability as he puts up with my crazy dreams and ideas. We have a two-year-old son, Jackson, who has inspired me to do my part to try to make this world a better place. We live in the Back Bay of my beloved city Boston, along with our Boxer Kendall, two cats, Yogi and Tess, and chinchilla, Bella.

Behind the Scenes

CALLING all RESCUES!

WANT TO BE FEATURED IN OUR FABULOUS
COFFEE TABLE BOOK?

Rescue advocate Brittany Bang of Audrey's & Boston pet photographer Li Ward of Fat Orange Cat Studio are teaming up to produce a coffee table book showcasing beautiful photos & success stories of local animals that have been given the greatest gift - a second chance!

WE ARE SEEKING PETS NOW!

Have a rescue pet? Contact Brittany for all the details (see the back).

100% OF PROCEEDS WILL BE DONATED TO AN ANIMAL CHARITY

THE PLANNING PROCESS WAS A LONG
AND ARDUOUS ONE, BUT SOMEHOW WE
MANAGED TO ENJOY EVERY COCKTAIL :)

ENCOURAGEMENT FROM
OUR MASCOT Bingley

TO BE CONTINUED...